BARCLAY BUTERA

LIVING ON THE COAST

BARCLAY BUTERA

LIVING ON THE COAST

GIBBS SMITH

TO ENRICH AND INSPIRE HUMANKIND

First Edition
16 15 14 13 12   10 9 8 7 6 5 4 3 2 1

Published by
Gibbs Smith, Publisher
P.O. Box 667
Layton, Utah 84041

Orders 1.800.748.5439
www.gibbs-smith.com

Designed by Sheryl Dickert
Printed and bound in China

Gibbs Smith books are printed on either
recycled, 100% post-consumer waste, FSC-
certified papers or on paper produced from
sustainable PEFC-certified forest/controlled
wood source. Learn more at www.pefc.org.

Library of Congress Control
Number: 2011942362

978-1-4236-2445-5

DEDICATION

As I reflect over the past eighteen years of my life and career, I have come to realize how important my relationships are to me. Without a doubt, I am truly blessed to have met the one person who has been by my side through every one of my successes and challenges; my dear friend Raymond Langhammer. Ray's unconditional loyalty, constant encouragement and incredible talent have all been major contributors to my accomplishments. His infectious laughter always helps to brighten my spirits and his family—Gramps, Mike, and Sharon—have become my second family and have been an amazing support over the years. When I started this business, I had no idea where this journey would take me; but with Ray along for the ride, the sky has been the limit. Thank you for all of your love and inspiration. We have achieved great things together and there is only more to come!

With love, Barclay

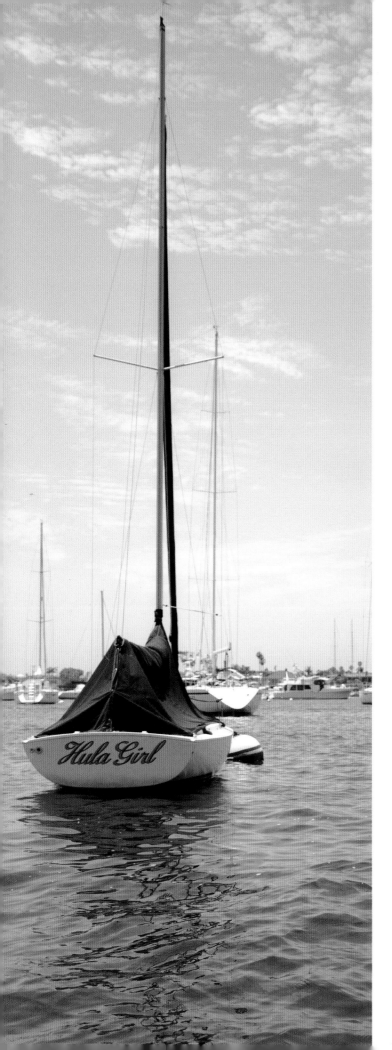

CONTENTS

SERENE BEACH

MODERN BEACH

ELEGANT BEACH

INTRODUCTION

As children, we're all taught that oceans cover 70 percent of the Earth's surface. To me, an even more compelling companion fact is that all of this saltwater has conspired to create an American coastline of some 6,000 miles, more than 12,000 miles if the chilly shorelines of Alaska are fully included. This seemingly endless ribbon where the sea meets the land, these beaches and shores and cliffs comprise an incredibly arresting American landscape: of deserted dunes and shingled houses, of fishing ports, of surf towns overrun with rambunctious young people, of elegant resort enclaves, of national parks. I love each and every local manifestation of life along the water.

From the rising and falling tides to the salt spray in the air and the magical quality of sunlight around water, very disparate coastal communities all seem to exhibit singular yet similar daily rhythms. In essence, there is a more gentle, more reflective and sensual quality to the coastline life.

My own particular affinity for the beach began in grade school, in the semi-hippie 1970s Palo Alto, on the sunny side of the San Francisco Peninsula. Any car trip over the famous area bridges or a simple glimpse of the San Francisco Bay itself served as a reminder, if any were needed, that just over the hill and through a patch or two of fog lay another world entirely, the Northern Californian coastline in all of its rugged beauty. Growing up, I became intimately acquainted with any number of quirky

beach towns along the old Coast Highway 101—from Half Moon Bay to San Gregorio and Pescadero and on southward, to surf-centric Santa Cruz, Monterey, Carmel and Big Sur heading north. For decades, like-minded beachcombers have washed up on the magical shores of the Pacific as well as the length of the Eastern Seaboard, the balmy curve of the Gulf Coast, the edges of the Great Lakes, the Outer Banks, and intra-coastal waterways and keys of Florida. Formality, structure and propriety seem to dissolve in proximity to the ocean. The rising and falling of its tides and unique beauty of its wildlife causes the senses to relax.

I eventually changed from day-tripper status to permanent resident when I moved to Southern California, living first in the artistic community of Laguna Beach and then eventually moved up the Pacific Coast Highway to Newport Beach, home to Newport Harbor, the largest recreational boat harbor on the West Coast. Living on this sunny stretch of the California coast, I became familiar with the eclectic nature of its visitors and residents: dreamers, artists, beach bums, surfers and sailors. The coastal lifestyle is a mixed cocktail of energetic water sports, sun-and-sand-induced lethargy, lively tourist traps, and the peaceful solitude of private waterside residences.

The aesthetics of seaside homes reflect a magical alchemy between the native and the exotic, the traditional and the whimsical, the mysterious and the familiar. There is a degree of artistic license that occurs within eyesight of open water. Practical considerations curb axioms of good taste to render what is now instantly recognizable as casual elegance. There is a more predominant use of wood near the coast; it has a softness and warmth that suits bare feet, wet hair, and sun-kissed skin. Furnishings are appropriately less ornate, and the pervasive presence of sand dictates a less cluttered and more casual approach to design.

Much accessorizing of beach homes is derived from the beach and ocean itself—driftwood, shells, beach glass, buoys—these objects reinforce that which is alluring about the seaside and naturally wear well in climates with an abundance of bleaching sunshine, corrosive salt, damp air and fluctuating temperatures. These conditions wear hard on home interiors. The drying wetsuit, damp sailing gear, the occasional tar on the flip-flops, an impromptu bar-becue for the next-door neighbors, extra house-guests and pets running inside and out all conspire to challenge any décor. It is challenging to integrate an auction-acquired antique or fine silk upholstery into a life amongst sun block, margarita salt, and endless summer sunsets.

Designs must, and do, happily adapt to this most treasured of lifestyles. Concessions are made and unexpectedly charming transitions occur. Painted pine pieces, sisal and more forgiving fabrics like linen attest to the game plan in play. The colors that look and feel great at the coast are simply those that are closest at hand: bright Mediterranean blue, cool celadon, salt white, and for a bit of punch—flag red. Crisply printed fabrics with boldly striped and patterned fields in these hues simply reiterate the color story and ambient excitement of a life lived at the coast—a somewhat rarified life of joy and movement and visual reward for those so inclined to follow the gaze seaward out the open window.

COTTAGE BEACH

COTTAGE AS STYLE

The term *cottage,* for me, is shorthand for small homes with a type of architecture that tends toward charming. Cottage style in North America involves a certain ambience to interior spaces that often includes built-in cabinets, cupboards, and closets and simple pine floors, which can be swept easily. Windows are ample, as the point of the coastal cottage is to embrace the natural environment.

Given the opportunity, most home hunters today would choose more space, more creature comfort, and more luxury than a small cottage offers. Anyone embracing a cottage aesthetic in this day and age is really demonstrating a personal preference for a less formal, less modern way of life. And I count myself among them.

I like a manageable amount of space with fewer and more utilitarian furnishings. I like the well-used look that cottages develop over the years. Everything pulls it own weight in a cottage. Anything fussy, out of place, or striking a false note tends to get broken or removed. Furniture is neither too large nor too small, as it needs to seat or sleep fun-seeking guests and their plus ones.

The memories of a cottage are of the experiences and excitement of the surrounding and not of any rarified decor. The cottage should be attractive, carefree and familiar. It should provide the pretty frame to happy memories of weekends away with the people we call our family.

LEFT: My very first beach home was formerly owned by screen legend Bette Davis, who purchased the house for her mother in the 1940s. The restoration of this vintage cottage was a formidable design challenge. To turn a 1,000-square-foot house into a livable home, I needed to reinvigorate the space without sacrificing the considerable period charm. The archetypal cottage appeal seemed to beg for an exuberant summertime treatment, so I went over-the-top with Americana furnishings that I sourced at antiques fairs across the country, from Brimfield, Massachusetts, to Burlingame, California.

ABOVE: Vintage white wicker dominates this comfortable outdoor seating area. The striped pillows and rug are flea market finds. The painted railing provides additional visual interest.

FACING: A jumble of fabrics in florals and patterns imbues the living room with cozy character. The versatile twelve-drawer chest from Barclay Butera Home creates essential storage space for household linen, blankets, and bedding. The Dutch door is quintessentially "cottage" and lends a charming, inviting element to a small home, not to mention considerable cross-ventilation.

ABOVE: Originally designed as a game table, the dining table with inlaid checkerboard centerpiece collaborates beautifully with floors painted in a black-and-white diamond pattern. The china cabinet is a custom piece, while the hutch was a great find filled with antique blue-and-white transferware. And as pineapples are the traditional symbol of hospitality in early American furnishings, the chandelier was a perfect fit.

BELOW: In the main bathroom, the lighthouse print and beachy accessories keep this small room playful. Painted beadboard wainscoting and blue-and-white-striped wallpaper add to a nautical theme.

RIGHT: The pitched ceiling is just one unexpected idiosyncrasy in the main bedroom. The window treatments are ribbon-tied curtains handmade from bed sheets. I continue the Americana flag motif in this room with antique pillows and a small bedside rug. I love the strong counterpoint of primary colors against soothing pale blue walls. Although I had the white four-poster bed custom built to fit the space, the white slip-covered "Somerset" sofa is current from Barclay Butera Home. Additionally, I gave the décor a boost of local color with framed prints from Laguna Beach artists.

LEFT: Like many homes near and on the beach, the front porch is merely an extension of the living space within. These capacious vintage wicker chairs are the perfect perch for people-watching or capturing a cool sea breeze. Flowering plants, baskets of shells, and potted topiary enclose the sitting area and add to the enticement.

ABOVE: A gardening station is clustered with tools, terra-cotta pots, and plants that are suited for coastal conditions.

RIGHT: This refurbished modern kitchen still retains its cottage roots—beginning with the painted tongue-and-groove ceiling. Glass-front cabinets allow colorful pottery to be seen with ease. An island provides additional counter space and storage, and the perfect vintage bamboo barstools snug up to the elevated bar top. The captain's wheel further buoys the nautical spirit.

BELOW: Louise is a cottage filled with vintage found objects; however, with more space to work with than in the Jasmine cottage, there's room for flair and flourish. Mixing hardwood furniture and flooring with a sisal rug and "Hurley" woven raffia club chair adds a super-textural dimension to the living room. The blue-and-white-striped slipcovered sofa, bamboo curtain rod and shades, and potted palm set a casual beach tone. Found signage and sailboat prints punctuate the wall space over the armoire.

Framed Art by Soicher-Marin (pages 20, 21, 23, 123, 161, 162, 194, 198, and 199).

FACING: Another perspective of the living area reveals a Dutch door behind a "Hurley" club chair woven from water hyacinth leaf and a blue-and-white ceramic lamp on a tiered end table.

ABOVE: This bedroom is a good representation of design symmetry. The round mirrors are reminiscent of portholes, creating a subtle nautical reference that fits in with the overall scheme of the house. Grasscloth walls, plantation shutters, and a ceiling fan with woven "frond" blades are tropical tropes. The use of fresh color—a pink-orange coral—in a medley of paisley, stripes and solids evokes exotic sunsets.

LEFT: The red, white, and blue palette extends to a tabletop. Even the grapes carry on the scheme!

FACING: This great gathering space was organized around an existing concrete table. I added brightly painted bistro chairs. I love the diamond-paned windows, which provide a fun architectural backdrop to this outdoor area.

South Pacific Shore

This room is a true living space for a large multi-generational family. Bold, deep sofas and pillows in blue and white exude a crisp, nautical feel. The sofa with nailheads—"Sussex," from Barclay Butera Home—is upholstered in white canvas and raffia, giving it a punchy two-tone quality, like a pair of spectator shoes—a fun take on a furniture basic. The sofa behind it is a blue velvet "Sussex" sectional. Reflective surfaces and glass accents contribute to the room's appeal.

A pair of sofas in deep oceanic blue provides a visual anchor to an otherwise light and airy open room. "Claire" ottomans from Barclay Butera Home introduce a touch of animal print. The lamp shade fabric and Chinese export porcelain continue the blue-and-white color story.

FACING: I love the contrast of the table finish with the rough texture of the sisal floor covering, seagrass window treatment, and raffia pillow. The chandelier shades are made from the same fabric as the paisley "Lido Host Chair" from my Home collection.

ABOVE: Blue-and-white Italian pottery, starfish-etched glassware, and hurricane lamps are perfect accomplices in this maritime-inspired tablescape.

ABOVE: By installing tile on the floor, I pressed this walkway into service as an ad hoc mudroom for sandy feet and wet bathing suits. Additionally, multiple cubbyholes of woven wicker baskets convert the space into a storage area. Storage is at a premium at the beach. You create it where you can find it. The oar coat hanger and starfish appointments add whimsical touches.

RIGHT: The bench cushion and pillows are sturdy striped canvas that evokes sailcloth. A small trestle table offers a charming pit stop for an impromptu bowl of chowder or cioppino.

PREVIOUS OVERLEAF: A soothing order is achieved in the master bedroom by the blending and layering of texture, pattern, and color: navy and white stripes, geometrics of blue and cream, woven raffia furnishings, and a floor clad in diamond-weave sisal. Floral pillows and an upholstered ottoman bring a tropical feeling into the room. A belt of windows provides expansive views all around.

ABOVE: The retro quality of the "Malacca" bed captures the allure of an exotic, enticing locale. Even a refined piece like a Barclay Butera Home "McKenzie" bench at the foot of the bed can find a home at the beach.

FACING: Nobody likes to feel left behind on a beach trip, so we made sure there was room for everyone! These built-in sleeping bunks make the most out of a very limited amount of space and add to the convivial shipboard atmosphere. The capiz shell light fixture and a simple rug on a hardwood floor keep the kids' room fun and relatively maintenance-free.

This sporty guest bedroom with its preppy palette is a rich contrast of navy blue and cream. The pillows add a punch of red, a color repeated throughout the house. The room is simply furnished with a mahogany bed and a striped "McKenzie" bench from Barclay Butera Home. Framed ship prints and a custom-made shell mirror enhance the maritime mood.

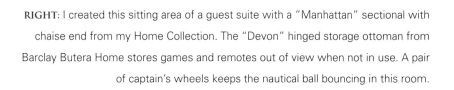

RIGHT: I created this sitting area of a guest suite with a "Manhattan" sectional with chaise end from my Home Collection. The "Devon" hinged storage ottoman from Barclay Butera Home stores games and remotes out of view when not in use. A pair of captain's wheels keeps the nautical ball bouncing in this room.

BELOW: In the same room, a daybed is accented with pillows in raffia and canvas. Playful red canvas stools with a shell pattern fit under a lacquered black coffee table and roll out for additional seating.

FACING: Resin wicker furniture and waterproof cushions outfit the deck for al fresco entertaining. This outdoor living room seems to float right over the dunes on a beautiful stretch of beach.

ABOVE: A pair of painted Adirondacks and striped umbrella placed just beyond the deck make a serene place to relax and enjoy the ocean view.

Pearl Cove

LEFT: A side street one block from the beach is home to this expanded bungalow getaway. Just about every interior space of this house opens to the outdoors—from the second-floor balcony and front porch to the rooftop deck.

ABOVE: The white painted front gate is a quintessential cottage element.

LEFT: The eclectic art works well here with patchwork fabric, anchor pillows, and a vintage needlepoint rug of a seascape. The black baby grand piano adds a touch of elegance. The "Hampton" sofa with T-cushion is from my Home collection.

ABOVE: The painted beamed ceiling keeps a guest bedroom open and breezy. Various shades of blue and white are at play in everything from the bedding and walls to the table skirt and window treatments. Red "Anchor" pillows are Barclay Butera for Eastern Accents.

RIGHT: True versatility is hard to pull off, but this large trestle table of pickled oak can accommodate formal or informal settings and graciously seats two diners or eight. A red striped dhurrie, patchwork cushions, and whimsical wall art lend energizing punches of color.

BELOW: An assortment of beach-inspired tableware makes mealtime fun and festive.

FOLLOWING OVERLEAF: The strong vertical of red in the living room enhances the architectural space. Seafoam walls and a floral rug provide the counterpoint of softness that keeps the room balanced.

CLASSIC
BEACH

CELEBRATING THE CLASSIC

At some point after World War II, the stereotypical beach cottage underwent something of a transformation. Prosperity pushed the envelope of the familiar, enchanting, and diminutive form known as the cottage.

While I do love the proportions and intimacy of traditional cottage spaces, I am no hand-wringer and, in fact, revel in the opportunity to design interiors for these more exuberant and ample spaces. Much of what I do with cottages is eminently applicable to these coastal dwellings writ large, but with more square footage, light, and wall space.

Extensive wainscoting, paneling, and crown moldings are possible in these rooms—architectural elements that really polish and refine the look. The typically higher ceilings and less heavily trafficked rooms mean that I can establish more formality to some of the spaces in a way that idiosyncratic layouts of cottages don't allow. Symmetry, balance, and rectilinearity are options as well, along with unique, somewhat ornamental pieces that are not compelled to multi-purpose and can simply serve more occasional use. A pair of full-length sofas is never possible in any cottage, but in these classically proportioned residences, I can create inviting and simultaneously commodious conversation areas and have room for lovely end tables and ottomans. Richer, more luxurious hardwood finishes like mahogany, ebony, and teak are less likely to overpower the generous spaces of these beach homes and yet aesthetically serve as exotic, nautical-inspired anchors for sitting and sleeping rooms.

The coastal classic house is just an amplification of the cottage vernacular: charming, useful, energizing—only more so.

Trouville

PREVIOUS OVERLEAF: Spaciousness and light are hallmarks of the classic beach home. In this living room, a Persian rug with bold colors and motif defines the seating area. Pillows in florals and stripes accent the cream linen of the Barclay Butera Home "Sussex" sofas and highlight the colors in the rug. A glass-topped coffee table and the Barclay Butera Home "Claire" ottomans in giraffe fill the space without crowding it.

ABOVE: Collections are a wonderful way to bring color to a room. Here, an abundant collection of vintage glass bottles topped with shells and coral fragments in shades of white, violet, and lapis pop against a soft-toned wall and a mirror from Barclay Butera Home.

RIGHT: The bones of the classic beach house include finely detailed wainscoting, crown molding, and dark, more formal wood flooring. Here a passageway has been converted into a gracious decorative moment with a "Davis" chair in navy blue and a custom "Calvert" console, both from Barclay Butera Home.

LEFT: An ornate shell chandelier with textural raffia shades collaborates perfectly with the tropical floral fabric of the curtains and bamboo shades.

ABOVE: The chandelier presides over a round "Raymond" dining table from Barclay Butera Home. The arrangement establishes a formal tone, while the colorful window treatments and shell lighting fixture "beachify" the space.

RIGHT: Bright throw pillows create contrast on the navy sofas. Nautical accessories are used in the room, but in a subtle way, to keep this house very classic. Light can be blinding at the beach, but here, doubling brightly striped roman shades over bamboo treatments works well to control it.

BELOW: A luxurious "Hampton" sofa in deep navy blue from Barclay Butera Home delineates the space between the kitchen and informal sitting area.

An architect has designed a contemporary interpretation of a rambling shingle-style Eastern Seaboard beach house from the turn of the last century. Deliberate quirkiness, such as an upper balcony trimmed in railing, multi-paned windows, and overall loose asymmetry, lends the house period authenticity and keeps it visually interesting.

Magnolia trees and potted topiary frame the Doric-columned front entrance portico.

RIGHT: A club chair in cheerful navy ticking is partnered with a navy leather club chair to define the sitting room adjacent to the kitchen. Unpainted rafters give definition to the ceiling and add rusticity to the space. Barclay Butera Home pillows in cream with coral graphics accent the chairs.

BELOW: Two signature pillows from Barclay Butera Home carry the sailing theme.

Because it's crisp, clean, and nautical, blue-and-white was chosen as the dominant color story for this beach house. Here in the breakfast nook, bent bamboo chairs with cushions made from bold blue-and-white lobster fabric surround a glass-topped bamboo table ready to be set with blue-and-white pottery and cobalt glassware.

Tall upholstered barstools at the counter seem like armchairs on stilts. Large blue-and-white Chinese porcelain urns and bright yellow accents give the mostly white kitchen energizing hits of color.

LEFT: This landing accommodates an occasional table with decorative nautical accents. The dark-finished wood table and handrails provide strong counterpoints to the creams and ivories of the stairway trim, balusters, walls, and bleached wood flooring. The stairway newel has been playfully re-imagined as a lighthouse. A focal point of the house is the stained-glass oculus window, custom designed with a flying blue-and-white spinnaker.

ABOVE: The use of dark, rich woods extends to a bathroom. A wall tiled in sapphire blue is instantly cooling, and whimsical shell and starfish elements keep the mood oceanic.

PREVIOUS OVERLEAF: In a bedroom suite, a curved window seat with raffia cushions has been customized for a pentagonal-shaped architectural nook to embrace the expansive marina view. A generous club chair is covered in blue-and-white stripe. Colorful accent pillows add punch.

RIGHT: The room gets its warmth and weight from a dark wood four-poster bed and matching nightstands. An enormous floor mirror in the same finish is propped casually against a wall. A pair of raffia pillows reiterates the upholstered Barclay Butera Home "McKenzie" bench at the foot of the bed.

BELOW: Two striped club chairs with bright red pillows dominate the foreground in this view of the bedroom suite. The vaulted ceiling painted in ivory contrasts with the dark neutral of the walls to create architectural definition.

LEFT: On the waterfront side of the house, an ocean gallery with glass-fronted walls becomes a year-round entertainment patio furnished with resin wicker chairs and table.

ABOVE: A view of the house from the private dock depicts its grandness, with its ample windows, decks, and second-story pentagonal turret facing the beach. A patio table and a built-in bench on the dock create an ad hoc gathering spot. Throw pillows make the improvisation festive and comfortable.

Via Lido Nord

FACING: This private dock in exuberant red, white, and blue juts out over the water. The flagpole is a riff on a sailboat mast. Wicker furniture, blue-and-white-striped cushions, red pillows, and a dazzling clear sky embody the spirit of a summer holiday on the coast.

ABOVE: A lovely brick terrace with potted tropical plants and a built-in bench overlooks a busy waterway, crisscrossed by serious sailors, day-trippers, and pleasure crafts.

LEFT: Under the terra-cotta-tile roof and Monterey-style open rafters, the terrace is a transition space to the outdoors. Adding natural textures are wicker chairs and settees upholstered in colorful blue-and-white regatta fabrics. Privacy cabana curtains are tied back to open up the setting and maximize the harbor view.

ABOVE: A rattan tiki bar occupying the other end of the terrace replenishes beverages. The bar and upholstered barstools provide overflow seating and gathering during family get-togethers.

FACING: This small study is a quiet retreat away from the bustle of the household. The "Colombia Lacquered Coffee Table" in Ming Red, from the Barclay Butera Lifestyles "City" collection, anchors the room. Underneath, the cotton floor covering is a fun riff on blue ticking. The antique American flag introduces a stately touch and, along with a model schooner, shells, and coral, forms an eye-catching display of old mingled with new and valuable collectibles alongside objects plucked off a sandy beach.

Westcliff Drive

FACING: Two "Hampton" chairs in navy with white welt, from Barclay Butera Home, create an intimate conversation corner. On the circular occasional table, a discreet glass lamp allows for an unobstructed view outside.

ABOVE: A group of vintage blown glass vessels corked with shells lines a sideboard. The brass lighthouse lamp juxtaposed with a framed sailboat print and red sailboat pillow sends the imagination off on an ocean cruise—without the hassle of having to stow a bag.

SERENE BEACH

SERENE BEACH: A SEA CHANGE

Plenty of coastal denizens, whether weekenders or life-long residents, escape to the beach for refuge and restoration rather than exertion and excitement. The balancing rhythms of the coastal environment—the rising and falling of a swelling sea, the pattern of chop on distant waves, the advance and retreat of a marine layer—tend to soothe and restore the more contemplative soul. A silent walk with the family dog or a fireside read is as close to "the source" as a morning in a wetsuit on a board.

I find that a subtle, more streamlined design aesthetic with a simplified, less contrasty color palette goes a long way toward enhancing a serene solace within which to reflect, repair, and refine the senses at the seaside.

The most natural and effective choice in creating this calming note is the featured use of a pale, cool colors. Soft aquas, celadon greens, light creams, and wan yellows are perfect complements to the abundant use of textural fibers like sisal, raffia, and cane. Less elaborate lines on sofa backs, armchairs, and side tables contribute to an overall tableau of spa-like tranquility. Glazed Asian pottery and lots of white—shells and coral, opaque ceramic and sheer fabrics, moldings and wainscoting—incorporate nicely in serene environments.

This design language is all of a piece to my mind, a seamless walk from room to patio to the natural world—coastal surroundings in which to immerse and consider, recharge and return.

Turnberry Springs

FACING: A shingle-style beach house opens up to ocean views, which are perfectly framed by windows and French doors. The furnishings of an outdoor sitting area carry on the mossy green color scheme of the home's shingled exterior. Throw pillows in solid celadon and an overscaled argyle pattern of celadon and cream complement the sofa fabric of striated pale green.

ABOVE: The entry hints at formality but is dressed down with celadon cushions on a weathered faux bois bench.

BELOW: A customized paint palette of lighter-than-air pale greens was developed for the interior of this coastal home. Tall windows welcome the sunlight, while an unbroken fall of curtain fabric accentuates the vertical space. A distressed glass-front wall cabinet displays seascape objects. The "Barrymore" woven club chair upholstered in a subdued pattern repeats the dominant hue of pale seafoam.

RIGHT: Cool colors of the shore—watery aquas, sea glass greens, and sand whites—segue inside to create a visual oasis in the living room. The Barclay Butera Home "Soho" leather cubes in jade discreetly provide extra seating.

ABOVE: The signature pale green wall color extends the oasis into the dining room. A table made from reclaimed timber, a glass-sided ceiling fixture, and "Kingston" leather host chairs from Barclay Butera Home transform the narrow space.

LEFT: Colorful abstract artwork provokes but doesn't disturb. Windows hung with celadon-and-cream draperies diffuse the light.

FACING: A breakfast nook is designed in muted tones of cream and seafoam. Simple beadboard-inspired built-in cabinetry, classically slip-covered linen chairs, and a pickled oak table collaborate beautifully to achieve a fresh, clean look. The absence of window treatments enhances the visual simplicity.

LEFT: French doors leading to an open terrace make this sitting room bright and airy. The focal point of the space—a mirrored Palladian window—adds dimension and drama to a room that wanted to feel larger.

ABOVE: The master bath is a spa-style space with a deep tub enclosed in a window niche. The tile flooring and countertop are a study in tones of sand and sea oats.

OVERLEAF: An upstairs bedroom embraces the refreshing spirit of the coast with beautiful, restful decor. French doors lead out to a balcony overlooking an unbroken vista of coastal pine.

LEFT: Under a pergola, cream-and-green chair cushions in broad stripes maintain thematic unity with the rest of the house and beautifully offset what already exists in nature.

ABOVE: A fountain feature just beyond the pergola provides the soothing sound of pooling water. Potted gardenia, palms, and climbing vines soften the outdoor architecture.

FACING: A loose asymmetrical approach to arranging strikes a balance in the family room, where raffia walls and sisal flooring warm things up. Cream upholstery fabric on the "Paris" club sofas from Barclay Butera Home takes a back seat to the pillows and dark woods of the mirror, frame, and Manhattan coffee table.

ABOVE: The master bedroom suite uses nature's color palette to mimic the tonal range found along grassy seaside dunes. The subtlety of sage and seagrass greens makes them easy to incorporate into interiors, where they almost function as neutrals. The Barclay Butera Home "Somerset" chairs are tufted in a seagrass-and-sand stripe.

Circle

LEFT: The striking symmetry of the dining room suggests formality, while cabinetry filled with antique china and a leather-trimmed sisal rug add coziness. Pagoda-shaped hurricane lamps reaffirm an Asian theme introduced by the silk-screened Japanese fan and kimono art on the walls.

ABOVE: A generous marble-topped prep island and dining counter is outfitted with black wicker barstools.

OVERLEAF: A delightful exterior sitting area is comfortably grouped with commodious chairs, a sofa, and ottomans. The water feature converts the shaded flagstone patio into a meditative retreat.

LEFT: Underscoring gracious formality, the exquisitely paneled living room is a vision of symmetry, balance, and texture in neutral tones of sand and sea oats. Pale blue-green pillows in watered silk delicately accent the Barclay Butera Home "Sussex" sofas. A soft area rug anchors the space.

ABOVE: A small adjacent dining area is defined by a delicate crystal chandelier above the table.

FACING ABOVE: Built-in shelving displays coral fragments, celadon porcelain, books, and photos.

FACING LEFT: The dining room sideboard shimmers with a collection of vintage hurricane lamps and apothecary jars.

ABOVE: A view from the sitting room into the kitchen reveals glass-front cabinets lit from within, a coffered ceiling, and expanses of lovely white marble. The Barclay Butera Home "Harbor" sectional in the foreground envelops a large leather ottoman. Behind the sofa, a "Raymond" square dining table from the Home collection converts the passageway between sitting room and kitchen into a dining space.

FACING: The positioning of the window and flanking built-in cabinets presents a unique situation that is resolved by centering the bed against the window. The cabinets obviate the need for nightstands. The paler-than-pale seafoam walls and soft floral pattern of the Roman shades promise relaxing, indulgent rest. A Barclay Butera Home "McKenzie" bench upholstered in celadon velvet and pillows in soft sea blue grace the room with vivid accents.

ABOVE: This creamy ivory bathroom is a color-free sanctuary. A soaking tub, a built-in marble vanity, glass pulls, diamond marble flooring, and a Hollywood Regency tufted chair add a dash of glamour to the room's spa-like tranquility.

ABOVE: In a powder room, a "Looking Glass" mirror in a heavy frame and grasscloth
walls add dimension and texture to this small space.

FACING: This problematic space is converted into a charming alcove with an
antique English chest accented with coral pieces. A framed sepia-toned photograph of a
listing sailboat keeps the moment nautical.

LEFT: A lower-level terrace opens onto a side courtyard and exemplifies the coastal interplay of interior and exterior spaces: it's not obvious where one ends and the other begins. Two distinct sitting areas are created in the expansive flagstone-paved, fireplace-crowned courtyard, which plays host to social gatherings throughout the year. Celadon pillows and floral prints are consistent with design elements echoed throughout the house.

BELOW: A landscaped pea gravel path beckons strollers to a headless winged sculpture at the garden's edge.

Ocean View

LEFT: The dark Barclay Butera Home "Regency" chairs create a more collected look and enhance the architectural space. The upholstered "Carmel" chair in blue-and-white ikat from Barclay Butera Home brings the colors of sand and ocean into this living room. Though only slightly formal, the room achieves a serene balance of luxury and relaxation.

ABOVE: Hurricanes and a collection of mercury glass vessels complement an ebonized mirror-glass chest. The oil painting of surf and rugged coastline adds drama.

Terrace

FACING: With the addition of a rustic mirrored chandelier and distressed dining chairs, the dining room becomes a cozy place to entertain.

ABOVE: Beyond the Barclay Butera Home "Sussex" sofa, a marble-top table and upholstered dining chairs create an old-fashioned eat-in kitchen.

ABOVE: The designer's affection for navy-and-white stripe extends into the guest bedroom of this serene beach home. The balance of the room is a thoughtful articulation of cream and sand.

RIGHT: Repeating the color scheme of the guest room in a downstairs sitting room, a "Sussex" sofa, "Somerset" chair, and "Devon" storage ottoman, all from Barclay Butera Home, give the room a comfortable spirit. This might be the best room in the house, with views spilling all the way down to the beach.

LEFT: Vintage paddles and a surfboard mounted on ivory walls plus a blue paisley comforter enliven this guest bedroom. It's fun to have one room that pushes the strong nautical theme.

ABOVE: An uncluttered, light-filled bedroom combines a celadon paisley spread with similar soft creamy colors of walls, rug, and sofa. Less contrast makes things restful.

FACING: Even the master bath is finished with rich architectural detailing. Paneled wainscoting surrounds the room; marble tile covers the floor. Tall French doors bring daylight in and open to a private terrace. A vintage claw-foot tub delivers a classic silhouette, while dark wood cabinetry provides a striking contrast to the shimmery atmosphere.

ABOVE: This distinctive Barclay Butera Home "Canton" chest graces a spacious hardwood passageway. The blue-and-white-striped cotton runner, Chinese porcelain pieces, and coral appointments are a timeless orchestration of Butera's coastal environments.

ABOVE: A replica hot air balloon basket has been converted into a tiki bar and stools. Tropical fabrics, island art, and exotic accessories make this rooftop cabana feel like a Polynesian retreat.

FACING: Vintage glass bottles, conch shell toppers, and a wood-carved pelican form a thematic collection on a vintage rattan tray.

ABOVE: Even the laundry room maintains the clean, ordered aesthetic of this home. A striped cotton rug flung across the marble floor provides necessary traction, while a toy sailboat and shells keep the space beachy.

FACING: This beach house merges architectural traditions from different regions and creates its own style. The shingles are reminiscent of Nantucket and Cape Cod coastal homes. The upper balcony is definitely Southern vernacular, while a first floor of open glass is de rigueur for a Florida beach house.

Cliff Drive

FACING: The rustic bamboo blinds and capaciously cushioned Barclay Butera Home "Somerset" sofa creates a cozy impression in this comfortable living room. The coral motif on a throw pillow adds a punch of color.

ABOVE: In the dining room, painted wainscoting circumventing walls of khaki not only sets off a focal point—prints of red coral—but also provides a dramatic backdrop for a long trestle table and chairs upholstered in neutrals and coral red stripe. A bench in marine blue provides adaptable seating. The bare hardwood floor keeps the room distinctly spare.

ABOVE: A kitchen accommodates dark rattan armchairs surrounding a round glass table, creating a favorite spot for meals, homework, and card games. Bamboo shades filter out harsh light.

RIGHT: Upholstered furniture in colors of dune, seagrass, and ivory create an inviting master bathroom. Accessories add strokes of turquoise and celadon to the décor.

MODERN BEACH

SYMMETRY AND THE SENSES

Sometime in the groovy seventies, a lot of modern architecture started springing up along the coasts. The vaulted ceilings and walls of glass were reflections of an incipient less-is-more design language coming into its own.

As a designer of interiors, I take much of my inspiration from the pre-existing architectural bones of the spaces I work with. I like to use a simplified palette with these soaring, double-height rooms, expansive open plans, and floating staircases. Instead of attempting to provide any sort of counterpoint to all of the straight lines, I tend to indulge my own fondness for symmetry and arrange simple-lined sofas, tables, and artwork in such as way as to reiterate the order of the rooms as originally conceived. Squarish club chairs, blocky coffee tables, and monochromatic rugs paired with fewer but bolder accessories are sympathetic furnishings. Minimal window treatments and ample use of glass-topped tables and glassy lighting fixtures celebrate the architectural light and space existent in modern homes.

There are still teak, raffia, and sisal, some playfulness in the upholstery fabric, and plenty of collected keepsakes and foundling beach talismans to make modern homes personal and warm. But overall these spaces are forward-looking and ahistorical in their incorporation of black, suede, and wrought metal. The complexity of the midcentury modern is relatively digested, but the yearning for a new order, an unencumbered future, is as fresh and vital as always. And I am as seduced by the perennial new leaf as anyone.

FACING: This contemporary living room seamlessly blends ornament and restraint. The open floor plan creates a rhythmic corridor that links living room to dining area to kitchen. The architectural cross-pieces provide recessed lighting and conspire with the low furnishings to create a visual field that is primarily horizontal. Barclay Butera "Soho" cubes in a free-form blue floral deliver color and pattern.

ABOVE: Another view of the living space reveals a boldly structural floating chimney that disappears into a vaulted ceiling. Striped curtains enhance this study in straight lines, which is relieved only by the curve of a nautilus shell and an oculus window.

Alta Vista Way

ABOVE: An over-large globe lighting fixture echoes the spherical pedestal table and the circle accents on the chair backs. High contrast is achieved through the juxtaposition of white walls and upholstery against darkly finished natural wood and window frames.

FACING: A grid of recessed wall niches, where fine porcelain pieces and other collected seascape objects are spotlighted, establishes a strong architectural presence in this living room. Celadon vases frame the Barclay Butera Home "Manhattan" sofa upholstered in warm cinnamon, a spice tone that complements the muted earth hues of the Oriental rug.

LEFT: An expanded color scheme on the bedding—bright golden blossoms, teal leaves, and a pale aqua background—evokes the shimmery palette of the Gustav Klimt painting. A Barclay Butera "Bel Air" bench in teal velvet provides a luxurious touch.

ABOVE: A contemporary curved porcelain basin defines this architectural bathroom. The travertine counter and sleek nickel hardware maintain the room's smooth and stylized tone.

ABOVE: Color is very important to the sense of feeling relaxed. Pale ice grays to cool, mineral blues collaborate with soft creams to dress the bed in a guest room. Over the bed, an abstract painting suggests infinite sky and descending sun.

FACING: A modern sculptural interpretation of the Renaissance fascination with the human form graces an exterior stucco wall. Nautical objects—vintage glass float, shells, seahorse, and tortoise—accessorize a weathered wooden bench. A dragonfly pillow adds a dash of flea market chic to the tableau.

LEFT: This modern residence is influenced by an Asian aesthetic. A strict organization of East and West furnishings imbues the living room with a refreshing layout of proportion and scale. A low Asian table charmingly communes with a Barclay Butera Home "Manhattan" sofa in a silvery gray velvet. Pillows in paisley, stripes, and solids reiterate the muted earth tones of the modernistic area rug.

ABOVE: Barrymore wicker club chairs square off across a low table with curved Japanese legs. Un-treated windows frame an unruly sea and soar to the ceiling.

Skyline Cliff

FACING: A china cabinet with bamboo fretwork panels echoes the square grid motif established by the front door and carried on by the kitchen cabinetry. The light fixture, dining table, and chair backs serve as circular counterpoints.

ABOVE: In this axial view of the dining area, only the delicate curve of the white phalenopsis disrupts the unwavering Asian symmetry and balance.

BELOW: A sculptural porcelain bathtub floats in an ebony surround. The floor is a grid of pavers and black beach pebbles.

A capiz shell pendant light fixture enlivens the open stairwell.

A landing area is appropriately large and filled with natural light. The floating staircase with custom irregular-diagonal zigzag railing is the centerpiece here, while the Asian folding screen and ebony settee underscore the sculptural quality of fretwork motifs traditional to Asian interior environments. A painting of koi fish coyly punctuates the Eastern influence.

RIGHT: Butera's coastal design work exploits as many opportunities as possible to draw in the beauty of the ocean. Sectional sofas in black wicker and white canvas create an outdoor living room that provides a commanding view of the coast from a cliff-side residence.

BELOW: A sweep of pool terrace is defined by a rough rock wall and a set of curved cutaway wicker chairs. Tiki torches and palm trees complete the tropical setting.

L'Auberge

LEFT: A flagstone porte cochere welcomes guests to this stylish boutique beachside resort.

ABOVE: The reception area is appointed with chartreuse velvet chairs and modern seascape wall art.

Del Mar

ABOVE: A "Manhattan" sectional sofa and "Madison" chairs from Barclay Butera Home create multiple conversation areas in the hotel lobby.

RIGHT: The beach setting is also implied in Butera's design choices. A breezy quality enhances the flow of cozy spaces that provides unimpeded access to beachside amenities. Potted topiaries pose in frozen profile.

Framed Art by Soicher-Marin (pages 20, 21, 23, 123, 161, 162, 194, 198, and 199).

LEFT: A bedroom suite with honeyed walls is furnished with "Paris" club chairs in chartreuse-and-cream houndstooth and a solid "Sussex" sofa, both from Barclay Butera Home.

ABOVE: Raffia adds texture to the room via the wall covering and the lamp shade on a modern pendant fixture. Framed vintage prints of palm trees above the headboard and tropical sham fabric collaborate to create a feeling of a vacation getaway.

OVERLEAF: The siting of the hotel provides magnificent views from every room and balcony. I designed this vast outdoor space to create a tapestry of distinctive sitting areas, connected by grass paths and dotted with native and exotic trees and plants.

ELEGANT BEACH

COLLABORATION

Often I find myself working with clients who have carefully acquired and curated valuable collections of furniture, artwork, and memorabilia. There is a level of connoisseurship among clients living along the coasts that is entirely related to travel. While it is something of a dream for any designer to work with an inventory of exquisite pieces already in the client's possession, incorporating them seamlessly into a newly designed space can be tricky.

The best collaborations with homeowner clients begin with our mutual selection and placement of a couple of much-cherished pieces, then I decorate around them. Most clients at this level have gained a deep appreciation for the luxurious hand of expensive fabrics and wall coverings, which can be used to highlight and showcase showstopping pieces such as sideboards, portraiture, chinoiserie, and porcelain. Richly colored textiles can provide exuberant backdrops as window treatments for European oak and walnut furniture and the exotic glazes and craquelure of Asian pottery.

While I love sisal floor covering for high-traffic areas, that in no way dissuades me from making use of enormous Persian rugs. Likewise the right incorporation of hand-tooled leathers, luxuriant linens, finely finished paneling, and eclectic accessories has an overall stunning effect.

Coastlines have historically been the crossroads where cultures collided and then ultimately cooperated. The result has been that delightful mélange of color, style, period, and tone not unlike the richly layered interiors that ultimately ensue from a chummy collaboration with a connoisseur client.

Shorewalk

LEFT: The furnishings in this Spanish Colonial Revival home are eclectic. A mixture of antique Asian and contemporary American pieces exemplify Butera's talent for layering seemingly dissonant styles and periods. Soaring vaulted ceilings, open rafters, and terra-cotta pavers are classic components of the Spanish Colonial Revival idiom. The home's design also provides practical solutions for a coastal climate: thick walls, large windows, and outdoor access in nearly every room.

ABOVE: Pillows featuring stripes, floral prints, and exotic motifs accent a refined "Canyon" wicker sofa. A blue-and-white porcelain lamp and ginger jar grace the adjacent antique sideboard of Chinese origin.

Harbor

RIGHT: A reverse view of the great room unveils a succession of arches that lead from one space to the next. All fabulous rooms draw you in again and again. Here, furnishings that resonate richness and splendor create a wonderful living and entertainment environment. Despite the capaciousness of the room, deeply cushioned sofas and club chairs create a warm, cozy feel.

BELOW: The jewel-colored Iberian fabric on the antique "Sorrento" Spanish Colonial chairs adds a touch of voluptuous elegance. Exposed upholstery nailheads and a hand-forged wrought-iron chandelier underscore the rustic feeling of this elevated conversation space created within the architectural margins of the great room. Similar curtains in both areas balance the amount of decoration. Through tall arched windows, shards of ocean are visible beyond the loggia.

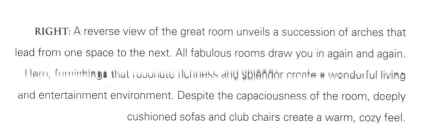

FACING: This elegant dining room opens to a sitting terrace. Rustic bamboo blinds serve
as a counterpoint to the elegantly carved fireplace and formal arched display niches. Above the table,
an ornate wrought-iron fixture drops from a coved ceiling. On the floor, vintage Mexican terra-cotta pavers
provide a foundation for the high style of Spanish Colonial Revival.

ABOVE: Just about every interior space has access to the outdoors, which pours in through each door
and window. A North African throw dresses a "Canyon" chaise in natural linen.

PREVIOUS OVERLEAF: Ruby red Burmese art glass on a large low table captures the radiance of natural light as it spills in through a plenitude of windows. The cardinal-and-cream floral curtains and pillows lend a tumbling air of profusion and color. A subdued Oriental rug further warms the room, which also features an elevated fireplace.

ABOVE: A spacious kitchen, a gathering place in any hospitable home, boasts an irregularly shaped oversized prep island. The granite top is repeated on the counters and backsplash. Pewter blue paint on the cabinets strikes a rich, unusual note. Atypical blown glass pendant lighting adds flattering function and visual interest to the large space.

ABOVE RIGHT: A generous Barclay Butera Home "Somerset" chair and ottoman are covered in brown-and-pale-blue ikat fabric.

BELOW: In the media room, built-in cabinets keep unsightly electronic equipment hidden.

ABOVE: Plantation shutters, an Indonesian cane bed, and the raffia fronds of a ceiling fan create a vivid trade route vibe. A spice trunk at the foot of the "Malacca" bed and a framed rattan floor mirror further provoke daydreams of exotic tropical getaways.

RIGHT: A study in the striking contrast of black and white, the master bedroom is furnished with an ebony four-poster bed from England, a zebra stencil bench, and a "Serena" chandelier. A bedspread in a drop-and-slip pattern of Rococo picture frames keeps the mood witty. Pillows and bedside lamps further salt and pepper the room with creamy white and crisp black accents.

PREVIOUS OVERLEAF LEFT: A simple room arrangement exemplifies a streamlined, livable design. The walls, floor, and fireplace treatment are kept neutral to allow pieces, such as the Barclay Butera Home "Somerset" sofa, to distinguish themselves. "Soho" cubes in zebra, from Barclay Butera Home, and a gilt-framed floor mirror add bold punctuation marks to an otherwise restrained, tailored backdrop.

PREVIOUS OVERLEAF RIGHT: A deliberate subtraction of decorative objects allows the artwork above the fireplace to be the focal point. As a result, the room communicates clean, fresh, and accessible elegance.

RIGHT: Four armchairs set on a bias surround an old-fashioned steamer trunk, forming a favorite spot for conversation or the odd card game. Identical appointments on an antique sideboard flank a mounted circular wall mirror and emphasize symmetry.

BELOW: The "Manhattan" sofa and "Devon" storage ottoman with leather top, both from Barclay Butera Home, occupy one end of a large sitting room. The red-and-white-patterned fabric of the Roman shades, curtains, and pillows punch up an otherwise neutral area.

Emerald Bay

ABOVE: This living room is a winning endorsement of laid-back sophistication. Two Barclay Butera Home "Sussex" sofas face off across a low coffee table. The accent pillows in stripes and paisley amplify the dark blue hues and swirling pattern of the Persian rug.

RIGHT: The insouciant juxtaposition of an antique mahogany table with vintage wicker chairs upholstered in vivid marine textiles gives this formal paneled dining space a comfortable, porch-like quality.

In a luxurious dining room, the clever use of toile on a pair of slip-covered dining chairs creates visual energy in a formal layout. A collection of Delft porcelain resides in a "Sutton" walnut hutch and enhances the blue-and-white color scheme. A lacy wrought-iron light fixture is the perfect accomplice to the delicate design of the fabric and china.

LEFT: A large arched window anchors a vignette with two Barclay Butera Home "Doheny" sofas and a pair of Barclay Butera Home "Claire" storage ottomans. Bold pillows in leopard fur and stamped alligator leather exude a touch of the exotic.

ABOVE: An antique dining table, leather upholstered chairs, and a rustic chandelier form a traditional dining room arrangement.

LEFT: The sun-washed European mood continues in this bedroom suite. The enormous sculptural archway subtly separates sleeping from sitting.

BELOW: One of a pair of graceful European antique chests serves as a bedside table next to an elegant bed frame. Gold tones of the antique frames and a tole ware planter contrast with many blues.

Vista Way

ABOVE: On a side table, an array of shells keeps the mood informal.

RIGHT: A Barclay Butera Home "Somerset" sofa and "Claire" storage ottoman reside in this casual den, made distinctive by the fieldstone fireplace and crisply painted coffered ceiling.

LEFT: An enormous leather sleigh bed with blue-and-white print linens stands out against crisp white wainscoting. This bedroom best reflects how cool colors and a dash of textured raffia can deliver seaside energy.

ABOVE: A bathroom cabinet depicts an innovative way to display household necessities with decorative objects. Nothing feels staged, just off-handedly arranged.

Carmen

LEFT: This light and airy room groups the Barclay Butera Home "Manhattan" sectional sofa in a corner. The textural "Peyton" ottoman, bamboo shades, and the deep oceanic blue of the upholstery weave the beach theme into the enticing room.

ABOVE: Chippendale chairs never fail to evoke a tropical mood.

Circle

RIGHT: The bedroom takes a more dramatic approach with walls covered in a sea of blue grasscloth. Sailing accents steer the décor. The goal here is visual comfort.

BELOW: The bathroom adjacent to a bedroom continues the aquatic color scheme with blue grasscloth walls.

FACING: This bedroom is inviting without being predictable. Walls of rich persimmon pump up the volume on the enduring color combination of blue and white. Beach priorities are reaffirmed with starfish piled in glass lamp bases and framed prints of shells.

ABOVE: The marble of the lovely Carrara floor tiles stays cool even in the hottest weather. Crisp, striped wallpaper in the colors of sea and sky creates a soothing order.

LEFT: The symmetry of this bright, bold living room confers a sense of traditional elegance, while beach-inspired objects and art make the formal symmetry fun. "Carmel" sofas and "Claire" storage ottomans in deep indigo from Barclay Butera Home collaborate with the red-and-white armchairs to keep the nautical spirit of the summer alive year-round. A painting of a crashing surf beckons us to the beach.

ABOVE: A raffia tray set with fresh flowers and carved pre-Columbian bowl forms an eye-catching display.

ABOVE: The siting of the house provides magnificent views from every porch area. Here, a loggia with overhead trellis allows for the dramatic pattern of light and shadow to arc, distort, and dissolve on the finely stuccoed exterior wall as the sun rises or sets on the coastal horizon.

FACING: The loggia is a transition space to the outdoors, with upholstered sofa and chairs in natural wicker, lots of greenery, and a flagstone terrace. Colorful accent pillows on navy canvas extend the red, white, and blue theme. Exterior wall sconces in oxidized iron articulate the space with a flourish of style.

ACKNOWLEDGMENTS

A special thanks to:

MR. AND MRS. BELJAK

MR. AND MRS. CREDLE

ANN AND GREG DENK

MR. AND MRS. FLANAGAN

DR. AND MRS. GUNN

MR. AND MRS. DOUGLAS HANES

ALEX HANSHAW AND THOMAS IRWIN

MR. AND MRS. KIRK HARMON

MR. AND MRS. WILLARD HARRIS

MR. AND MRS. HOUSSELS

RAZA PASHA, M.D.

LIZ AND MIKE RUDINICA

TAMIE RUS

MR. AND MRS. SHAMALEY

MR. AND MRS. PETER J. SHEA

DR. AND MRS. SOWERS

And thank you to all my friends and staff, including:

CHERIE LUNA

CHRISTINE PHILLIPS

SAM AND TIFFANY SLATER

RAY LANGHAMMER

KRISTIN MARIE MORRIS

SUDI JELVEH

LOIS ICHIKI

CALEB JONES

ASHLEY DANG

MEL BORDEAUX

Photography by:

MARK LOHMAN – INTERIOR PHOTOS

ASHLEY DANG – LIFESTYLE PHOTOS

Barclay Butera has based his career on a passion for beautiful yet livable design. Butera's mantra of redefining luxury has not changed his firm belief in helping his clients achieve the "Better-Best" concept of living. The end result has been a consistent redefinition of home décor luxury and interiors: glamorous and completely approachable. His interior and exterior environments are based upon the philosophy of layering diverse styles of furniture, textiles, and textures.

With his licensed partnerships—Kravet Textiles and Carpets, Bradburn Lighting, Eastern Accents Bedding, Merida Natural Fiber Rugs, Mirror Image, Nourison Carpets, Wendover Art Group, and Zodax Home Décor and Fragrance, in addition to the Barclay Butera Lifestyle furniture line (BARCLAYBUTERALIFESTYLE.COM), Butera has made his unique style available to the consumer wanting to add a touch of glamour to their home.

BARCLAY BUTERA SHOWROOMS

BARCLAY BUTERA INTERIORS

WEST HOLLYWOOD

918 North La Cienega Boulevard
West Hollywood, California 90069
TEL 310.657.0882

NEWPORT BEACH

1745 Westcliff Drive
Newport Beach, California 92660
TEL 949.650.8570

PARK CITY

255 Heber Avenue
Park City, Utah 84060
TEL 435.649.5540

WWW.BARCLAYBUTERA.COM